www.booksbyboxer.com

No part of this publication may be reproduced or transmitted in any form or by any means, electronic or mechanical, including photocopying, recording or any information storage and retrieval system, or for the source of ideas without written permission from the publisher.

Bee Three Publishing is an imprint of Books By Boxer
Published by
Books By Boxer, Leeds, LS13 4BS, UK
Books by Boxer (EU), Dublin, D02 P593, IRELAND
Boxer Gifts LLC, 955 Sawtooth Oak Cir, VA 22802, USA
© Books By Boxer 2025
cs@boxer.gifts
All Rights Reserved
MADE IN CHINA
ISBN: 9781915410962

This book is produced from responsibly sourced paper to ensure forest management

1. Some joker switched my ball for an egg.

2. The Earth's magnetic field flipped mid-swing.

3. Neptune swung into Capricorn, shifting the hole three feet south at the last minute.

4. My shot was flag-bound when the greenkeeper deflected it with his rake.

5. I mistakenly teed off with my golf umbrella.

6. You win some, you lose some, I suppose.

7. The factory must have countersunk the dimples on my ball.

8. There was an earthquake; my ball fell into a sinkhole.

9. The groundsmen are usually tidy, but roadkill on the 18th?

10. A jet stream blew my ball off its perfect line.

11. I'm an Aquarius, golf isn't our preferred sport.

12. I had my golf shoes on the wrong feet.

13. I had the sun in my eyes.

14. One of the guys swapped my ball for a ping-pong ball.

15. I nodded off mid-swing.

16. I accidentally did my croquet swing.

17. My golf bag got stolen, I can't stop thinking about it.

18. I thought 140 yards was a tad long to sink with a putter!

19. My shrink thinks I have developed a fear of making par.

20. The sun reflected off my bald partner's head, into my eyes.

21. I tried to align my swing with the horizon and took my eye off the ball.

22. I was still laughing at the mess I'd made of the last hole.

23. Must lose weight; can't see the ball for blubber.

24. I forgot to take my shoes off to be more grounded for my shot.

25. That shot would have been perfect on WiiSports.

26. My scarf was too tight.

27. Being over par is my hobby.

28. It was my evening to cook and I was preoccupied with whether to make fish or meat.

29. An acorn had gotten into my sock.

30. A traveling circus had set up on the fairway.

31. The grass conspired against my lie.

32. A Jehovah's Witness tried to enroll me on the fairway.

33. I thought I was trying to make a 30-foot putt instead of 3 inches.

34. I used a kitchen mop instead of a driver!

35. My lucky tiepin malfunctioned.

36. I got distracted by a squirrel.

37. I used a tennis ball instead; what was I thinking?

38. The ball is clearly unbalanced.

39. I misread the humidity today.

40. A bug flew into my eye.

41. I heard someone sneeze.

42. I think I hit a buried rock.

43. I used a bowling ball instead — I know, crazy, right.

44. Gravity must have wobbled.

45. That divot wasn't there a moment ago!

46. I was lining up my next shot early.

47. My partner's shadow put me off.

48. Somebody replaced my golf ball with a ping-pong ball.

49. I had a sweaty glove.

50. I was distracted by the beverage cart.

51. I hit a root.

52. My shoelace was loose.

53. I was thinking about my last putt.

54. My ball's GPS failed.

55. I heard a bird chirp and it distracted me.

56. I was due a bad shot.

57. I lost my balance.

58. I forgot to account for the change in Eastern Standard Time.

59. I forgot to stretch before playing.

60. The voices in my head told me to fluff the shot - who am I to argue?

61. A hummingbird hovered over my ball, and I was overwhelmed by wonder.

62. My club head hit a blade of grass at the wrong angle.

63. I was aiming for the scenic route.

64. I had golfer's toe.

65. The ball is obviously defective.

66. I played a divot instead of the ball.

67. I should have used my lucky ball.

68. That was my safety shot.

69. My golfing trousers were too flamboyant.

70. The tee marker was aiming in the wrong direction.

71. A fly landed on my ball just before impact.

72. I accidentally used my buddy's club.

73. My golfing socks were too tight.

74. A sprinkler head threw me off.

75. I accidentally hit a worm burner.

76. I got caught between a fade and a draw.

77. I swung too fast.

78. I was distracted by my beautiful reflection in the water hazard.

79. I was dazzled by my own brilliance.

80. I was trying to lay up.

81. I misread the fairway, I thought it broke left.

82. I never played from a lie like that before.

83. I should've practiced more.

84. I was distracted by my opponent's ugly shirt.

85. I think my club face was open at impact.

86. I forgot to adjust my stance.

87. I hadn't taught my ball how to fade.

88. I swear the tee box is uneven.

89. I should've taken an extra practice swing or five.

90. My knee cracked mid-swing.

91. I got a golfer's cramp in both ears.

92. My partner looked at me funny.

93. I forgot to adjust for the slope.

94. I didn't stretch my wrists enough before taking the shot.

95. I was afraid of hitting the ball too far.

96. I was swinging too aggressively.

97.   I had skipped breakfast.

98.   I forgot to reset my grip after my practice swing.

99.   I was thinking about lunch at the turn.

100.   I was trying to give my opponent a chance.

101.   I was in putting mode.

102. My opponent's luminous golfing socks distracted me.

103. Someone zipped up their golf bag too loudly.

104. I warmed up too much on the range beforehand.

105. That bunker was just too tempting.

106. I tried to hit a low punch shot but forgot to hit the ball.

107. My new swing adjustment is still a work in progress.

108. The course designer had a bad sense of humor.

109. My ball has a mind of its own. It's a rebel.

110. I'm telling you, that ball jumped up in the air!

111. I was too focused on my follow-through.

112. I forgot to rotate my hips.

113. My club face was both open and closed.

114. I thought I was using a different club.

115. I caught the ball a little thin. Okay, a lot thin.

116. My ball is afraid of the fairway.

117. I wasn't hacking through the rough; I was practicing chip shots.

118. I was actually aiming for the rough to challenge myself.

119. Perfect hit, wrong direction.

120. I was distracted by someone jingling change in their pocket.

121. A spectator sneezed just as I teed off.

122. I'm never good on short grass.

123. I was standing too close to the ball after I hit it.

124. My ball only knows how to slice.

125. That was a promo that mere mortals do not understand.

126. My golf clubs wanted to humble me.

127. That was a classic case of club face confusion.

128. I actually hit the perfect shot but it was for another hole.

129. A classic case of overthinking.

130. I didn't want to hit into the group ahead so I hit into the group behind.

131. I was distracted by my own pure ability.

132. I was playing for the big bounce but forgot to tell the ball.

133. I don't know where those trees came from.

134. That is what you call a smart miss.

135. I got too excited and rushed my swing.

136. That was a controlled miss - just not well-controlled.

137. I hit the wrong part of the ball.

138. The fairway is far too narrow.

139. My caddy handed me the wrong club

140. I forgot to transfer my weight.

141. My ball had plans of its own.

142. I zigged when I should've zagged; what can you do?

143. That was a strategic miss - just don't ask me the strategy.

144. I forgot to factor in the morning dew.

145. I forgot to take into account the solar wind.

146. What? When you bend your knees you should bend both at the same time?

147. I overestimated the slope of the fairway.

148. I expected better from a $10 driver.

149. You pay $15 for 12 dozen balls; you need new ones in six years! Sheesh.

150. Well, that's golf for you!

151. I was caught between two clubs and picked the wrong one.

152. I was aiming at the pin but my ball was aiming at the bunker.

153. I caught the ball too clean.

154. Bad pin placement in my opinion.

155. The wind stopped just as I was planning for it.

156. My trousers were falling down.

157. The green slopes more than it looks from back here.

158. There must be an underground spring because that water obstacle wasn't there a few minutes ago.

159. I'm worried about hitting someone's house so I hit someone's car instead.

160. I misjudged the wind by about 50 yards.

161. I was worried about duffing it so I thinned it instead.

162. I didn't notice I was standing on a downslope so I didn't adjust.

163. I tried to play the wind but the wind played me.

164. The wind was blowing at right angles.

165. I was demonstrating the weekend hacker chunk.

166. I felt a raindrop and panicked.

167. They must've been using the fast-growing grass.

168. The pins have been set up unfairly today.

169. My socks were too tight.

170. My scarf was too tight.

171. I was testing out a new ball.

172. I hit a tree limb that must've grown overnight.

173. I didn't want to under-swing so I over-swung.

174. I looked up too soon.

175. I feel like my face was open, closed, and sideways all at the same time.

176. I got nervous because a flock of geese seemed to be plotting something.

177. The ball refused to listen to my mental instructions.

178. My partner was standing in my peripheral vision.

179. I was distracted by a goose having a stare-down with me.

180. I was trying to avoid hitting a duck.

181. A dog barked just as I started my backswing.

182. I had my weight on the wrong foot.

183. A chipmunk was watching me and I felt under pressure.

184. I had to adjust my stance because of an anthill.

185. My caddy knows nothing about golf.

186. I was trying to impress my group.

187. The hole was too small; shouldn't there be regulations about this sort of thing?

188. The ball jumped off the club face in a way that defied physics.

189. I was distracted by a duck leading its ducklings across the fairway.

190. A bee flew up my nose just as I started my downswing.

191. I was aiming for the green but my ball was aiming for a swim.

192. The grass has never liked me.

193. I was playing for the wind - turns out the wind wasn't playing.

194. I thought we were playing crazy golf.

195. A raccoon stole my buddy's ball and I couldn't stop laughing about it.

196. The water hazard was far too close to the fairway.

197. My back locked into place as I prepared to take the shot.

198. My glove was on a backward.

199. I was aiming for the middle of the green but my ball disagreed.

200. Thought it was a hydration shot, my ball was thirsty.

201. I thought my ball was waterproof.

202. I heard a golf cart backfire.

203. The group behind us was singing army songs loudly.

204. I heard someone unwrapping a snack in the middle of my shot.

205. A crop duster flew overhead just as I played my shot.

206. I haven't had my shot of coffee yet.

207. A leaf blew across my ball right before impact.

208. It can't have been easy with the grass growing in the wrong direction.

209. I think I slept wrong, my neck is locked up.

210. Someone in the clubhouse was playing music too loud.

211. I was thinking about what to have for lunch.

212. The grass was unusually thick today.

213. I got distracted, wondering if I'd left my car unlocked.

214. I stayed up late watching golf videos, which clearly didn't help.

215. That was a planned mishit.

216. I thought I saw lightning and my fight or flight instinct kicked in.

217. My hands are too cold.

218. The winds are no friend of mine.

219. I could hear the group behind us betting on whether I'd slice my shot into the trees.

220. I got a sudden cramp in my toes.

221. I blinked when I shouldn't have.

222. I forgot to drink my energy drink.

223. My knees felt weird.

224. I forgot to warm up.

225. Mercury had just gone into retrograde.

226. The course is 100 yards too short for my optimal game.

227. I think my contact lenses decided to swap eyes at a critical moment.

228. I was dizzy from all my triple bogeys.

229. The sun blinded me.

230. My hand slipped - too much lotion, not enough grip.

231. I lost balance when my left foot fell asleep.

232. The green was far too green for good golf.

233. I miscalculated the Earth's gravitational pull.

234. I was testing how far the ball could go into the trees.

235. I was too busy thinking about what Tiger Woods would do.

236. My left arm forgot to stay straight.

237. It was the golf club's fault; I can't be responsible for everything.

238. I forgot to wear my lucky golf pants.

239. I meant to whack the ball into the river.

240. My schedule distracted me at the last moment.

241. Oh, you wanted a putt, not a drive!

242. The fairway wasn't wide enough.

243. My fingers went numb from gripping the club too hard.

244. The course is three trees short of the official minimum.

245. Sometimes you have to screw up to give your opponent a chance.

246. I am allergic to success.

247. A squirrel was staring at me judgmentally.

248. I sneezed at a crucial moment.

249. Someone coughed in the distance.

250. My putter and 3-iron are haunted.

251. I lost focus while stifling a sneeze.

252. The course is 3in^2 short of the regulation area.

253. My body and my brain weren't on speaking terms during the swing.

254. My opponent deliberately stepped into my peripheral vision. I am allergic to success.

255. A dragonfly distracted me.

256. At the critical moment, my opponent said "You need to make this one count."

257. My chakras were all over the place.

258. There was a piece of half-chewed gum sticking to the ball.

259. I shouldn't have tried swinging with my eyes closed.

260. My club was aerodynamically flawed.

261. My opponent whispered the wrong yardage to me.

262. My opponent complimented my swing right before I hit - instant jinx.

263. My opponent asked which club I was using and it made me second-guess myself.

264. My grip was too slippery.

265. My opponent slipped me a fake helpful tip just before I swung.

266. The sprinkler soaked my golf trousers.

267. My opponent whispered "Don't shank it" right before my shot.

268. I was playing too fast.

269. My opponent gave me the quiet stare of doom while I was over the ball.

270. I was so confident that I closed my eyes. It didn't pay off.

271. My hands were far too relaxed.

272. 100 practice swings was probably one too many.

273. I was playing too slowly - almost in slow motion.

274. I forgot to factor in the wind resistance of the grass.

275. I forgot to take my sunglasses off.

276. I did it again; I misread the altitude pressure at sea level.

277. The golf cart horn honked of its own accord.

278. The ball had mud on it.

279. My golf ball wasn't qualified for tournament play.

280. My plan was perfect until I swung.

281. I was aiming for the other ball.

282. I misjudged lie - and everything else.

283. I was distracted by thinking about what I'd order in the clubhouse.

284. My shades misted over.

285. I accidentally used my hockey slap shot.

286. I swung in metric instead of imperial.

287. I was trying to play smart but couldn't remember how to do that.

288. I was distracted by how dazzling my new golf outfit was.

289. I got stuck between 'go for it' and 'play it safe'.

290. I adjusted for a wind that never blew.

291. I was thinking about how to celebrate my next birdie.

292. The ball was exhausted; it had had a busy week.

293. A butterfly flew right into my backswing.

294. My caddie forgot to charge my good luck charm.

295. I was practicing my foul shots to appreciate the good ones.

296. I was still thinking about the three I had on the last hole.

297. My alignment was perfect for another fairway.

298. That gust of wind came out of nowhere.

299. I got bad advice from a YouTube video.

300. My golf shoes weren't broken in properly.

301. A grasshopper heckled me.

302. I was distracted by my boyish good looks.

303. I mistook my practice swing for the real one.

304. I made perfect contact with the ground.

305. I swung too fast for reality to keep up.

306. I was trying a new technique.

307. The wind was blowing backward.

308. I was waiting for the ground to settle under my feet.

309. My putter has performance anxiety.

310. A molehill disrupted my stance.

311. It was far too cold.

312. It was far too hot.

313. I was aiming for a comedic effect.

314. I was worried about embarrassing myself.

315. I tried to visualize the perfect shot, but my brain wasn't up to it.

316. I told myself to trust the process and the process betrayed me.

317. I was playing so well, something had to go wrong.

318. I let my ego take the swing.

319. My hands were too dry.

320. The course was designed for taller players.

321. I was worried about what my buddies would say about my shot.

322. A gnat flew up my nose.

323. It was so foggy I couldn't see the end of my club.

324. A sudden earthquake shifted the ground beneath me.

325. My golf bag is heavier on bad days.

326. My swing speed dropped off because I'm wearing too many layers of clothing.

327. My shoes didn't have enough grip.

328. The breeze made my eyes water.

329. The wind stopped just as I adjusted for it.

330. My ball plugged in a wet fairway.

331. I miscalculated the angle of success.

332. My fingers slipped from overconfidence.

333. My ball was still spinning from my last shot.

334. I was distracted by my opponent's good shot.

335. I was standing on an uneven lie.

336. I underestimated how bad I could be.

337. My body pointed in one direction and my feet in another.

338. I was too bent over. I felt like I was playing mini golf.

339. My swing was set to "random."

340. 'Don't think, just swing' is good, but there has to be some thinking.

341. My lucky golf shoes ran out of luck.

342. I thought I was playing baseball.

343. My watch is on so tight it's cutting off the circulation to my strong wrist.

344. I thought I was in a bunker but I was in the middle of the fairway.

345. My shirt was so tight, I couldn't rotate properly.

346. My shirt was too loose and it got caught on my backswing.

347. My golf ball is a rebel — it doesn't follow the rules.

348. My belt was digging into my stomach.

349. I mistook my slice for a signature move.

350. I was standing on a mega divot.

351. I put it in the bunker to practice my desert survival skills.

352. I'm just following the golf god's orders.

353. It wasn't a duff shot; it was an unconventional strategy.

354. My socks were sliding down inside my shoes.

355. I forgot to breathe out before the swing.

356. A sudden itch seized my left nostril.

357. I put it in the bunker because it's a shortcut.

358. I like the scenic routes.

359. Did you see that seagull? It was huge!

360. I remembered an excellent joke mid-backswing.

361. My shoes were so tight, I couldn't feel my feet.

362. Who laughed just as I took the shot?

363. Overconfidence from an excellent practice swing.

364. My underwear was bunching.

365. Knocked my ball into the trees because I was aiming for shade —it's hot!

366. I don't know what happened, but it definitely wasn't my fault.

367. I knocked my ball into the trees because... the wind swung suddenly treeward.

368. Knocked my ball into the trees — thought I saw a shortcut through the forest.

369. My golf shoes creaked at a crucial moment.

370. My ball's in the pond because I was trying to wash it.

371. I knocked my ball into the trees because the fairway was too crowded anyway.

372. That wasn't a bad shot, the course is just unfair.

373. I was working on my trick shots.

374. I forgot which way the hole was!

375. It's not my fault if the ball doesn't go where I aimed.

376. I felt the ghost of Seve Ballesteros tap me on the shoulder.

377. My ball is in the pond because I wanted to see how waterproof it is.

378. That was a practice swing. I just happened to make contact.

379. The ball spun too much - obviously a factory defect.

380. That water hazard wasn't there yesterday!

381. I didn't get it out. They just put the boundary in a bad place.

382. I'm just giving everyone else a confidence boost.

383. I've been practicing at mini-golf; the windmill isn't here to help me.

384. My ball moved only 6 feet because that was just a warm-up shot.

385. I didn't want to scare away the insects in the grass.

386. I was checking the ground level.

387. I was testing my tree ricochet skills.

388. Someone glued my ball to the tee!

389. I just got my clubs regripped.

390. My ball moved only 6 feet because the grass was too tall.

391. I had a hard day at the office.

392. My ball barely moved because I was weak from laughing at my previous shot.

393. I wanted to give everyone time to admire my form.

394. I didn't hook it - the fairway just isn't in the right place.

395. This ball needs more air in it.

396. I got a little too excited and swung early.

397. It was an optical illusion - it looked way worse than it really was.

398. Well, everyone has a different strategy.

399. My ball moved only 6 feet because I aimed for a low-runner shot.

400. My ball moved only 6 feet because I prioritized precision over power.

401. The wind hates me.

402. Gravity seems to be stronger on this course.

403. It's harder than it looks to hit a perfect 6-foot shot!

404. It wasn't me, my equipment failed me.

405. My ball moved only 6 feet because I was testing the club's sweet spot.

406. If not for that one bad bounce, it would've been perfect.

407. I was helping conserve golf course grass.

408. I'm trying to invent a new swing style.

409. That tree wasn't supposed to be there.

410. The ball doesn't respond well to my coaching style.

411. I thought golf was supposed to be a walking game, not a playing one.

412. I refuse to accept that shot as part of my score.

413. I was distracted by the beauty of the course. Nature calls, you know?

414. My ball moved only 6 feet because gravity was unusually strong right there.

415. My caddie gave me the wrong advice...

416. This is all part of my master plan to hustle everyone later.

417. My warm-up swings were just too good; I peaked early.

418. I thought the goal was to explore every inch of the course!

419. There were too many bumps on the ground.

420. I just realized I'm left-handed... halfway through the round.

421. I left my talent at the driving range.

422. I didn't know that bunker was in play.

423. I didn't want to embarrass the course record holder.

424. My new strategy is slow and steady is best.

425. The grass isn't cut to my exact specifications.

426. I'm trying to record the most mulligans in one round.

427. I don't want to intimidate anyone by playing well.

428. The grass is uneven – it's the groundskeeper's fault.

429. I'm just following the 'hit it where they ain't' philosophy.

430. I didn't lose my ball. Someone must have picked it up.

431. I don't trust this course.

432. I thought the water hazards were bonus targets.

433. I enjoy the sound the ball makes when it lands in the water.

434. The scoreboard is a liar. I played much better than that.

435. I was aiming for the tree to use it as a backboard.

436. I thought we were practicing trick shots.

437. I was aiming for the other hole, so I technically nailed it.

438. That wasn't a duff, it was a strategic mishit.

439. My ball moved only 6 feet because I didn't want to show off too much.

440. The grass grabbed my club. It had no chance of escaping.

441. I was distracted by the sound of someone else's good shot.

442. I'm practicing my recovery shots... a lot.

443. My hair was in my eyes.

444. I hit the shot perfectly. It's the result I'm not happy with.

445. My swing is so advanced it's ahead of its time.

446. I'm trying to turn golf into an extreme sport.

447. The sun reflected off my club at contact, blinding me.

448. I thought it was sitting up, but it was actually buried.

449. I'm trying to build character, one bad shot at a time.

450. It was a divot - should be a free drop if you ask me.

451. I saw a cat eyeing up the ball, thought I might as well make it a good chase.

452. The rough was thicker than it looked.

453. The grain didn't do what it was supposed to do!

454. I'm not bad at golf; I'm just good at making it enjoyable.

455. I thought I'd try get it in the next course's hole to speed things up a bit.

456. I just remembered I left the oven on at home.

457. I wouldn't have made that pot if the green hadn't been lying to me.

458. I forgot to do my lucky ritual before I took the shot.

459. I'm training for a competitive worst-golfer competition.

460. I just wanted to show you how not to do it.

461. I slipped just before the shot - this course is not up to code.

462. I read somewhere that a lousy golfer lives longer... so I'm playing it safe.

463. I could swear I felt the tectonic plates shifting.

464. The rain fell in my eyes, I couldn't see.

465. My shoelaces are done way too tight.

466. I didn't want you to feel worse about yourself than you already do.

467. I needed to mess that up to humble myself.

468. I need to regrip my club's handle.

469. I figured the odds are that if I mess up this shot, you'll mess up yours too.

470. The tee markers are pointing in the wrong direction!

471. The odds were stacked against me.

472. Did you just see that lazer? I think there's a sniper aiming at me.

473. You can't win 'em all.

474. I guess I was just flying too close to the sun.

475. Jeez, this trapped gas is really cramping my style.

476. My glove slipped a bit on the backswing.

477. I must have picked the wrong club.

478. I saw an unusual shape in the clouds and it distracted me.

479. Don't speak to my ball - you're making it go the wrong way.

480. I worked out too much and and the club is too light for my arms.

481. Is this hole regulation size or what?

482. I mustn't hit it too far — safety first!

483. That cart took off right in my backswing.

484. I shot the wrong distance with my range finder.

485. Someone's chewing gum too loud.

486. That was a 'flyer' - the ball must have been a little too bouncy.

487. The wind just picked up out of nowhere.

488. I let the ball decide where it wants to go. It chose poorly.

489. I took the perfect shot from this position on this hole back in 1991 - I've been trying to recreate it ever since.

490. I read an article about creative golfing and took it too seriously.

491. I don't want to set unrealistic expectations for my next round.

492. It felt like I was swinging with a wet rag.

493. I whiffed on purpose - just thought I'd get a practise swing in.

494. There was people celebrating loudly on two fairways over.

495. The group in front of us is too slow. I have to keep waiting and it throws my game off.

496. I got an important text as I was swinging.

497. There is a nudist colony on the other side of the small lake. You can't see anything, but you can hear them partying.

498. It's too cold. Every time I hit the ball my hands hurt because the club is stiff and the ball feels like a rock.

499. A mini tornado blew my ball into the pond.

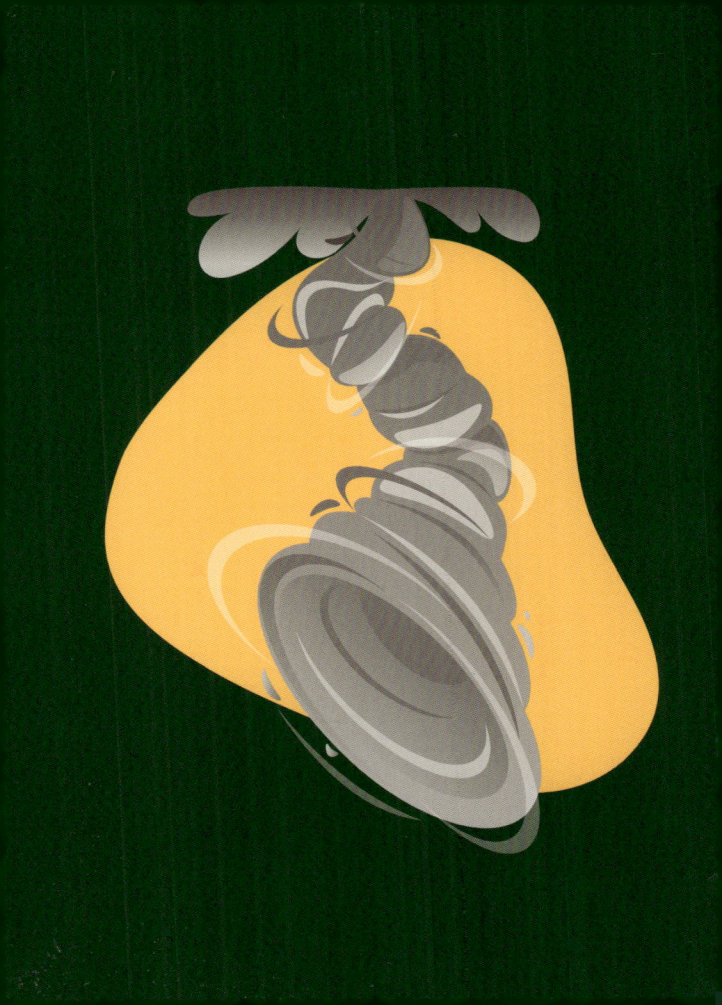

500. A squirrel ran across the fairway right as I was swinging.